POCKET IMAGES

Arnold & Bestwood

Richard Parkes Bonington, 1802–28, is believed to have been born on High Street (formerly known as Back Side) in the premises now occupied by the local Labour Party. Shortly after Richard's birth the family moved to Nottingham, and then, in 1817, to France where his artistic talents were soon recognized and developed. Today Bonington is considered one of the founders of the English School of Art. Poor health ended his short life and he was eventually buried with his family in Kensal Green Cemetery, London. In 1911 a statue was erected to him at the School of Art in Nottingham but the weather was unkind to the material used and by 1945 it was moved to the Castle Museum, and the canopy to Arnot Hill Park. In 1992 the statue was obtained by Gedling Council. Restored, it is to stand in a place of honour in the Civic Centre.

POCKET IMAGES

Arnold & Bestwood

M. W. Spick

NONSUCH

First published 1994
This new pocket edition 2007
Images unchanged from first edition

Nonsuch Publishing Limited
Cirencester Road, Chalford
Stroud, Gloucestershire, GL6 8PE
www.nonsuch-publishing.com

Nonsuch Publishing is an imprint of NPI Media Group

British Library Cataloguing in Publication Data.
A catalogue record for this book is available from the British Library.

ISBN 978-1-84588-467-3

Typesetting and origination by NPI Media Group
Printed in Great Britain

Contents

Central Arnold from the air, 1972. Although the street patterns remain, a number of them are now cul-de-sacs and buildings once familiar to the residents are already a memory.

Royal occasions. Although the area was visited in earlier times when Bestwood was a Royal Hunting Park, the first official visit came on 21 October 1983, when Princess Alexandra opened Moira House and visited the new library.

Introduction

The story of Arnold began in the sixth century as the Anglo-Saxons invaded the east coast of England and settled along the banks of rivers such as the Witham and the Trent. One such settlement was at Arnold, then known as Ernehale. The first record of Arnold, however, is not until the Domesday survey of 1086.

In 1436 it was recorded of Arnold that there were 'divers' (various) houses and buildings 'greatly ruined' and 'worth nothing'; the plague had also spread into the village.

Situated north of Nottingham, Arnold remained a poor agricultural region until the Industrial Revolution. Then the invention and growth of the stocking frame and lace manufacture, as well as the introduction of the factory system in the 1870s, caused the decline of agricultural and cottage industries. Competition from nearby Nottingham and surrounding villages also had a detrimental affect on Arnold and by 1854 the village was so devastated that an appeal to Parliament resulted in the formation of the Local Board, the forerunner of the Urban District Council in 1894.

From the start it was a constant struggle to respond to the challenges of creating a better standard of living, and matters were further delayed by world events. Trade and monetary difficulties also caused unease. The village grew southwards into a town and despite the monotony of long discussions, improvements were gradually achieved. The town was supplied with gas by 1858, but the main priority was to provide a good supply of water. This was not achieved until 1872, when pipes were finally laid; the last of the hated water bucket closets, however, did not disappear until 1955. After the Second World War a concentrated effort was made to bring about improvements designed to help the residents and cope with the new influx of people.

Since 1898 efforts have been made to incorporate Arnold into Nottingham, but without success. The boundary changes in 1974 meant the end of an independent Arnold (and Bestwood) and the creation of the Gedling Borough. At the time of writing, however, everything is 'on hold' once more as new boundary changes are being proposed.

Princess Anne, Mrs Mark Phillips, opens the new Civic Centre, 1 November 1985.

One

Pretty as a Picture

Before the introduction of the Edwardian topographical postcard the main visual record was that created by the often amateur local artist.

This postcard, dated 1902, conveyed a very popular message.

The Lodge Farm Guide House, Redhill, drawn by Miss E. Smallwood in 1930. The house was known by travellers on the road to the north as early as 1562. There are many anecdotes connecting it with Charles II and Nell Gwyn. Demolished in 1978, only the front wall is left as a reminder.

Arnold Academy, 1883. This drawing of the Academy, which disappeared shortly after the Second World War, was used to illustrate the pupils' exercise books. The stricter, simpler form of education is very different to today's.

The Smithy, Blatherwicks Yard, as it appeared in 1925 (top) and the same scene in 1994 (below). The artist is W. Orgill.

Bryants Farm, Front Street, painted by an unknown artist, 1878. The farm stood at the corner of Ravenswood Road.

St Mary's church and the top recreation ground, painted in 1900 by Mr Nightingale as a background for Mr Impey's cow, Sue. The animal was so prolific in her milk yield that she was eventually honourably retired and spent the rest of her life at Dorket Head.

The orphanage near Redhill Road, 1920, painted by Miss E. Smallwood. It was built in 1887 and demolished in the early 1920s to make way for other developments.

A painting of the top of the town showing the parish church from Surgeys Lane, painted by Stacey-Blake (1873–1964), and presented to the author in 1955. The artist lived in Arnold from 1920 until his death.

St Mary's church. Recorded in the twelfth century, the church was restored with Victorian thoroughness in 1870–2. The line drawing above shows the 'new' church in 1872, while the lower one was drawn in 1942 by Stacey-Blake as a Christmas card.

Swinehouse Farm off Scout Lane (now Woodthorpe Drive), painted by A. Barnes possibly in 1915. The area is mentioned in the history of the village from its earliest times.

Sandfield Road, painted by Sybil Fisher in 1911. Known as early as 1790, this is now a highly desirable residential area. Although the cottage on the left still stands, its future is very much in doubt.

St Mary's church from Pondhills, painted by Miss E. Smallwood in 1930. It is difficult to appreciate that the village was first 'industrialized' as long ago as 1770.

Bulwell Field, painted by Miss E. Smallwood in 1930. This was a popular walk, even if the old workhouse was at the end of the path.

St Pauls church, Daybrook, built through the generosity of Sir C. Seely. These two line drawings show the original building of 1890 (above) and the interior of the main church opened in 1895 (below). The spire was added in 1897.

The Black Swann, Woodthorpe, painted by an unknown artist at the turn of the century. The drover in the picture is said to be 'Cock Oliver', a well-known local character.

THE MEADOW SCHOOL

Meadow School, Nottingham Road, sketched by the author in 1957. This unpretentious building was erected in 1790 and used as a chapel, school, Chartist HQ, storeplace and a council yard before its demolition in 1965.

Brookfield Road. This undated picture by an unknown artist shows an area that was once known as Washpond Lane. A bleach works stood near here in 1832.

Gambles Farm, Calverton Road, painted by Miss E. Smallwood in the early 1930s, has only recently disappeared under urban redevelopment.

Church Drive East, painted by W. Wheatley (1893–1977). This section of the road was created between the wars and joined Mansfield Road and Nottingham Road, Daybrook.

Front Street, *c.* 1915, on a postcard used as a jigsaw puzzle.

Two

Other Faiths

By 1993 the old parish of Arnold contained three parish churches, two Roman Catholic churches, one Methodist and three Baptist churches and a number of other faiths.

St Timothy's church, Daybrook, was created in 1993 to replace Cecil Hall, an annex for St Paul's church. Behind it stands St Alban's Primary School, opened in 1961 to replace the old school on Mansfield Road, Daybrook.

The Assembly of God, Furlong Street, 1953. Begun in 1951 by the Nottingham City Temple and meeting originally in a 'mobile church caravan', the church moved to the old Salvation Army Hall in 1953. This is a view of the original building, which has recently been enlarged.

The Christian Spiritualists, Mansfield Road, Daybrook, c. 1955. This movement started meeting in an upstairs room in this old factory building which became vacant when the Catholic movement moved to Thackeray's Lane. Today a DIY superstore occupies the site.

Above: Coppice Road, c. 1957. A number of religious faiths held their first meetings in the yard of this property at the corner of Front Street and Coppice Road.

Right: The Salvation Army Hall, Coppice Road, in 1912. This is part of the property shown above. The Salvation Army first visited Arnold in 1879 and fluctuated between here and New Basford until 1930. Revived for a time in the 1930s, the faithful travelled to Nottingham. The Salvation Army currently meet in what is now the Old People's Centre, but property has been purchased on High Street to be developed into a new all-purpose building.

The Wesleyan Reform Church, Burford Street. The Reform Church met in an unused factory until the 'tin' church (above, about 1958) was erected in 1898. A 'temporary' building, the tin church was to stand for sixty-seven years until the present one (shown below about 1968) replaced it.

Many events and social occasions revolved around the various churches, including, of course, football. This photograph dates from the 1906/7 season.

The Jehovah's Witness Hall, Furlong Street. This group first met in a building on High Street in 1940, moving to Coppice Road in 1943 until these premises were built. In 1993 the structure shown here was altered and enlarged.

The Congregational Church, Calverton Road, in the mid-1920s. The Congregationalists came from Addison Street, Nottingham, in 1870, although their first meetings were held at Queen Street. A year later the church above was opened and in 1938 a new one (shown below in the late 1950s) was completed. Between 1923 and 1939 a men's institute was built on Arnot Hill Road.

The Congregational football team, 1907/8 season. An ever-popular game, most churches and societies supported their own teams.

A keep-fit class held by the Wesleyans in 1913.

The Prophecy of God, Church Drive, moved into the old Methodist church in 1969 and catered for a newer, more distinctive and lively congregation.

A Whitsuntide demonstration outside the Church Drive church, 1902. The orchard which stood there can be seen. The houses in the background are on St Alban's Road.

Other well-supported groups are the Scout movement (top) and the Boys' Brigade (below), seen here marching at the rear of the old British School on Front Street. The school was demolished in 1956 to make way for a market. Both photographs date from the late 1950s.

Whitsuntide demonstrations between the wars. Started in the last century, the popularity of these demonstrations grew steadily until 1977 when the pace of progress and lack of support made it difficult to continue with them.

Whitsuntide demonstrations in the 1950s. On the great day one never knew whom one would meet (right) but all came together for the opening service, held since 1925 on the bottom recreation ground (below).

Whitsuntide demonstrations. Two views illustrating what was the main event of the year for the town. Above, on Nottingham Road near the Bonington Cinema, c. 1960. Below, on Mansfield Road, Redhill, c. 1925.

Whitsuntide demonstrations in the 1970s. While the opening service was being held, the decorated vehicles were judged, many reflecting the issues of the time, such as the float above from 1971. The final parade was in 1977 (right) on the King George playing fields. One mystery remains— what happened to all the competitive cups and shields that were won?

Whitsuntide demonstrations in the mid-1960s. Whatever the significance to others, it was a day that the children, even the smallest (above), could really enjoy. The inclement weather (below) was no deterrent.

Whitsuntide demonstrations. However tiring it became, straight backs, smart marching and happy smiles were the order of the day.

The declining level of interest is evident from one of the final walks, c. 1975. Note the buildings behind, now completely altered.

In the early 1980s May Day parades replaced the Whitsuntide parade with folk groups from far afield taking part and collecting for charity (above). A visiting team from Ghent in Belgium created great interest (below). Lasting for ten years, progress and business interests once again caused their demise.

Three

Keep the Home Fires Burning

There was an old miser who said
'I keep all my cash 'neath the bed'
But one Blitzy night
It all caught alight
Now he puts it in savings instead.

Wartime propaganda

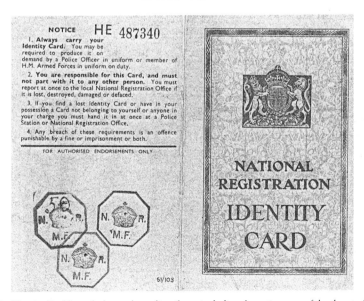

The Identity Card brought home the reality of war, including the seriousness of the threat of invasion, which would turn the country into a front line fortress.

Local men quickly rallied to our defence, and there were many from Arnold and Bestwood in the 8th and 9th Battalion of the Sherwood Foresters in 1939.

ARP Wardens Post, Sandfield Road. These cheery volunteers are, left to right, Messrs Stacey, Lockley, Cone, Gates and Sulley.

Hammond's Garage, Mansfield Road, shown here in 1926, was taken over and used as a fire station. It was not returned to its former used until 1949.

More fund raising for the war effort. Dick Turpin (A. Stacey) holds up Mr Gee, in the tall hat, and Mr S. Hammond in 1941.

ARNOLD WAR WEAPONS WEEK!

———

(Arnold, Calverton, Daybrook, Woodborough
Lambley, Redhill, Woodthorpe)

———

MAY 17th–24th
1941

OPENING
CEREMONY

SATURDAY, MAY 17th
ARNOT HILL PARK
3-0 p.m.

———

CHAIRMAN:
THE MARQUIS OF TITCHFIELD, M.P.
(The Lord Lieutenant of Nottinghamshire)

Arnold's answer to the call for support.

Right: Another fund raising effort organized by, left to right, Messrs Lockley and Stacey in 1941. The third person is unknown.

Below: The Methodist school, Worrall Avenue, c. 1965. The school building was used as a British Restaurant. The mind boggles when one learns that the potato peeler had to be placed next to the toilets.

METHODIST CHURCH, :: HIGH STREET, ARNOLD.

SUNDAY SCHOOL ANNIVERSARY

SUNDAY, APRIL 6TH, 1941.

PREACHERS :

Morning 10-30,
REV. CYRIL NEWMAN

Afternoon 2-30,
REV. G. R. TRUSSELL

Evening 6-0,
MR. L. T. WOOTTON

SINGING AND RECITATIONS BY THE SCHOLARS.

ANTHEMS BY THE CHOIR.

Conductor :
Mr. J. DOVE.

Organist :
Mr. J. W. DOVE

Despite the difficulties, everyone tried to keep to a normal routine wherever possible.

Local men assemble on Trent Bridge cricket ground, c. 1940. They faced an uncertain future.

Recently modernized, this old factory at the bottom of St Alban's Road was used for military purposes for allied troops stationed in the area. The photograph dates from 1993.

Left: Arnold supports the Navy.

Below: Redhill Lodge, 1943. The Lodge was used by the RAF during hostilities.

GERT AND DAISY TAKE PART IN THE FUN

Above: Boosting morale. Elsie and Doris Waters, the well-known entertainers, judge the ladies' ankle competition at the Arnold, Daybrook, and Woodthorpe District Nursing Association sports gala. One wonders if the magnifying glass helped.

Right: Clarke's factory was one of many geared to victory, in this case producing rolling stock for the railways. Mr Burdett, standing alongside his machine, is said to appear on occasions as a spiritual guardian.

Clarke's factory, Coppice Road, commenced in 1879 (above). The works' personnel on the eve of war work in 1937 (below).

ARNOLD'S THANKSGIVING
VARIETY SHOW

DRILL HALL, ARNOLD,
MONDAY, OCT. 1st, 1945,
7.45 p.m.

```
*********** ********** ****** *****
*                                 *
* ALL STAR PERFORMERS SELECTED    *
*                                 *
* FROM LOCAL TALENT CONTEST.      *
*                                 *
*********** ************** ******
```

TARGET

£50,000

Produced by A. L. Stacey for Committee
URBAN DISTRICT of ARNOLD
THANKSGIVING WEEK
29th SEPT., — 6th OCT., 1945.
CHAIRMAN...... ...... REV. H. BUSHELL

Fletcher, Wilford Gres. E., Nottm.

The war was fought with a ferocity and cruelty very few realized, but when peace came in 1945 everyone was very grateful.

Fund raising efforts took many forms. This incident occurred outside St Paul's church, *c.* 1946.

Victory was celebrated everywhere with street parties. This one was on Nottingham Road, 1945.

The R. Mellors School scholars holding their own peace celebrations in 1946 at the Empress Cinema (above) and at the school (below).

Crowning the Victory Queen in 1946. Miss I. Bailey is crowned by Mr W. Locksley at the climax of the day's events held in typical English weather—heavy rainfall.

The inscription on the War Memorial in Arnot Hill Park. This is the only known acknowledgement and written record of the men of Arnold who paid the supreme price.

Four

Sir John Barleycorn

Brewing is an age-old tradition and in 1875 John Robinson began the business in Arnold which thrived so successfully it was taken over by Scottish and Newcastle in 1986. Sir John Barleycorn is the popular traditional name for brewers.

Sir John Robinson was the youngest child of Thomas Robinson. Born in 1839, he was educated in the village. He helped in the family business, and on his father's death he took over the malting business, purchasing land to expand from the Duke of St Albans in 1865. In 1877 he founded the brewing industry and named it Home Brewery after their farm in Bestwood. In 1882 the original buildings were opened. The business was so prosperous that by 1890 Sir Robinson was able to buy Worksop Manor and other properties. His wealth enabled him to mix in many social circles, carry out moral duties and hold offices in the county. Retiring on the death of his son in 1898, Sir Robinson was knighted in 1905. He became a great benefactor to many causes, and died in 1929.

Home Farm, Oxclose Lane. This was the farm from which the business took its name and where the grain for brewing was grown. This photograph was taken about 1956, shortly before the building was demolished.

The farm on Cross Street where the brewing began, 1990.

The original frontage to the Home Brewery, Mansfield Road, *c.* 1930. In 1904 the mineral works were added and in 1926 the Killingsley Spirits were purchased.

The construction of new premises was started about 1935 but work was interrupted by the war. This photograph was taken about 1965. The panels between the windows show each stage of the brewing process. The clock, which was originally intended for the tower, was found and installed in 1994.

An aerial view of the brewery before its modernization. Travelling clockwise from the top left the surroundings include Coronation Buildings, which replaced a row of cottages in 1937; the unfinished new offices behind which can be seen the show house never used; the laundry and the Old Spot Inn; Folly Row, bottom right; the Apollo Works, now the Killingsley Dept; and on the left side the back-to-back houses on Portland Street. When Newcastle and Brown took over in 1986 it serviced 447 public houses, 6 clubs and 17 off-licences.

Home Brewery workers. An early transport parade (above, c. 1935) and the annual outing to the east coast about to depart from the old railway station at Daybrook in 1936 (below).

The Lord Nelson, Front Street, is first recorded in 1841. In 1923 a distinctive frontage in green tiles was added. This photograph dates from about 1965.

The Old Spot, Mansfield Road, Daybrook, 1992. First mentioned in 1744, the establishment was known as the New Inn in 1782, but as the Old Spot two years later. This view, taken from the top of the brewery offices looking west, also shows the laundry, and some of the developments that have taken place over the last forty years.

The White Hart Inn, Mansfield Road, Redhill, was known in 1765 and used for a turnpike gate in 1787. (The gate was moved in 1802 after a long dispute.) Much business was arranged here, and many outings set off from the inn, like the one shown above about 1910. In 1964 the old building closed and a new one was opened (below). Note that all the other properties have now disappeared.

The Vale Hotel, Thackeray's Lane, 1964. The hotel was opened in 1938. On the left can be seen the old railway bridge, which was demolished in 1966.

The Flying Horse, High Street, 1955. First known as the Friendly Tavern in 1832, the inn changed its name to the present one in 1850. The cottages at the side have been replaced by a pool hall.

The Robin Hood and Little John, Church Street, first known in 1765 and shown here during the early 1920s. For some unknown reason the 'Little John' part of the name, included as early as 1802, was omitted from all information until 1934.

The Friar Tuck, Gedling Road, 1970. Opened in 1958, the Friar Tuck is one of the very few so named in the country.

The Severn Stars, Calverton Road, is marked on a map of 1791. Like all taverns it was a social centre for a variety of activities. It was closed in 1969 and is shown here shortly before demolition.

Last orders at the Severn Stars, 1969.

Five

As Time Goes By

This section recalls some of the day-to-day activities of the parish, and some of the changes which have occurred.

Front Street, 1912. Today this street is completely modernized and pedestrianized. In *White's Directory* of 1864 No. 40 is recorded as 'A neat police station built in brick in 1861 and containing two cells'.

No. 15 Church Street was the site of the manor of Arnold. About 1790 it was demolished and replaced by this Georgian building, which was used for many years by the medical profession. On the right-hand side was the original Smithy Row, first mentioned in 1797. The photograph dates from 1955.

The Parker family take afternoon refreshment, 1900. The house stood until 1928 when it was purchased by Mr Nix the builder. The new manor house was built on land opposite known as Home Close at the same time as the old manor house was pulled down.

The manor house which was built in 1928. The central front window was purchased from the Exchange, which was also being dismantled from the Market Square, and the old city coat of arms can be seen from this interior view (below). Both photographs were taken in 1993.

A parade of the local militia in 1910, probably in connection with the death of Edward VII, created great interest.

When this aeroplane landed at Dorket Head during the air race round Britain in 1911 it attracted hundreds of sightseers.

Excitement of a lesser kind was encountered at the school sports day. Parents participate (above) while onlookers encourage them (below) in an event which took place shortly after the Second World War.

Daybrook station (shown above in the early 1950s) opened in 1876 with the Suburban Line added in 1889. The photograph below, *c.* 1910, indicates that the station was well supported, but good road communications limited its success.

WAITING FOR THE TRAIN.

Daybrook station after a fire which occurred in 1914. The cause of the disaster is unknown.

Daybrook station area in 1994. The station was situated to the left of the picture although all traces of it have gone. The Bero Works on the right was built in 1932. At the time of publication a DIY premises is being built on the space in the foreground.

Local sports were very popular, especially on the top 'rec' (above) near St Mary's church, shown about 1930. The King George playing fields (shown below about 1980) were a welcome addition.

Football was very popular and there were a great many teams made up of local lads like these.

This team of St Mary's were Notts Senior Cup winners. Back row, left to right: Molynex, Gough, Ironmonger, Simpson, Parr (Capt.), Anthony, Gregory (trainer). Front row: Moore, Leverton, Coombe, Gray (mascot), Collindridge, Williams.

Front Street from High Street in 1934 (above) and the same area in 1994, now renamed The Green (below).

The Carnegie Library (above) opened in 1906; the photograph dates from 1980. Today the site provides facilities of a different kind (below).

The following poem was written by Mr Spray, of West Street, Arnold, who was then the choirmaster at Front Street Baptist church. It was recited at the Front Street Baptist Christmas Concert in 1897 by Albert Corah, who then also lived in West Street, Arnold. The poem contains the names of all eighty-eight shopkeepers in business in Arnold at that time.

Advertising Arnold

I have a little picture,
I wish you all to show,
Altho' some of you present,
Will all this picture know.
Well spose you stand on Bestwood
Or top of Dorkett Head,
Or on Red-hill about the arch,
Or Mapperly hills instead
And cast your eyes around you,
From East, West, North and South,
You'll see a great big valley
Resembling a huge mouth.
Well in this vale is Arnold,
That nestles rather low,
Midst fields & trees & hedges,
And brooks that gently flow.
You get to it from Mansfield
Or Nottingham at will
From Mapperly or Woodborough
By going down a hill
As some here may be strangers,
To you I will unfold
A little information
What Arnold now does hold.
There's Chapels, Schools and Churches
There's streets and roads and lanes
There's Banks to save your money
And Tradesmen:– Here's their names,
   Extalls, Flowers & Watkins,
   Weatherhalls & Fleet,
   Doves, Starbucks, Clovers,
   Are where the roads do meet.

Tansleys, Randfords, Yates,
Pembletons & Dean,
Palethorpes, Wards & Hartshorne
In the front area seen.
Booths, Archers, Showels,
Alcocks, Hearsons, Jews,
Brailsfords, Monks & Woodcocks,
Goldstraws for the news.
Roses, Franks, Williamsons
Ellis, Clay & Fells,
Marshalls, Woods & Blankleys
Stones and Kenniwells.
Foster, Holts & Trumans,
Grettons, Barnets, Moores,
Orange, Smith & Palletts,
Stimsons, Spencers, Stores.
Sturton, Crump, Parr, Naylor,
Saxton, Cooper, Cooks
Hufton, Surgey, Burrows,
Pearsons for your boots.
Turtons, Holbrock, Skerrits,
Bradshaw, Saywell, Scotts
Kirk, Hammond, Beeton,
Bostock for your pots.
Wardles, Fish and Fisher,
Storeys, Needhams, Manns,
Hopkins, Pecks & Shepherds,
Will shave you when he can.
Jacksons, Mees & Oscrofts,
Mellors, Briggs and Ball
Herrings, Cliffs and Bramleys.
A Merry Christmas to them all.

The Croft in the 1960s. The entrance with Mrs Paviers' shop can be seen on the left, and the Horse and Jockey (known as the Horse and Groom by 1797) stands on the right.

The Wakes were held on the Croft until 1963 but traffic problems and other alterations caused their demise. This photograph shows the event during the 1920s.

Above: The Croft today, now known as Croft Road. The Health Centre, which opened on High Street in 1990, is at the top of the road. The space in front of it and to the right is used as a car park.

Right: Bumble Bee Cottage stood opposite Cross Street Baptist church. This tiny one-up and one-down dwelling was a classic example of how space was utilized during a period when the town was developing rapidly. It is shown here in the late 1940s and was demolished in the 1950s.

Above: The Fisheries, Daybrook Square in the early 1950s.

Left: Lucas's on Portland Street, 1932. The shop moved to Oxclose Lane about 1957. Mrs Lucas, Joan, Bill and Steve are looking on.

Right: The chip shop on St Alban's Road. In 1946 there were twenty-six such establishments, and a 'tuppenny mix' (chips, peas and fish bits) was considered a banquet. Today a wider variety of food is sold and the prices have also changed—a fish costs £1.65 (£1 13s) and chips 65p (12s 6d) and 90p (18s).

Below: In 1978 the first hypermarket appeared on Front Street – an example of how facilities were being provided for the area, but at the expense of other property (see p. 78).

Moira House, Front Street, originally the country home of a former viceroy of India. This view, photographed in 1865, shows Dr Allen and his family. The medical profession used the house until it was demolished to make way for the hypermarket shown on the previous page.

Dr Francis's car, driven by Mr S. Williamson, was a familiar sight in Arnold between the wars.

A charity stall, Front Street, 1957. The fourth person from the left was K. Negus, the local librarian, who with a dedicated staff created one of the finest comprehensive libraries and local pictorial records in the area.

The Cross Keys, Front Street, c. 1920. Known by 1780, it was here that the Local Board of Health first met in 1854.

Above left: In 1853 the Oscrofts (William and John, left) brought an All England team to play Arnold. The match attracted several thousands of spectators, reflecting the popularity of the game at this time.

Above right: G. Anthony (1876–1907), a well-known local man.

Cricket has remained a popular sport and local teams like these (bottom left included) from the 1950s gave much pleasure.

In 1892 the local constabulary (above) and Inspector Bishop (left) dealt with a variety of problems. Inspector Bishop lived from 1865 to 1959.

In 1989 a traffic policeman halted a bus to Arnold and found 131 people and 3 dogs aboard. It was allowed to proceed but forty-eight of the passengers had to walk the rest of their journey. The incident was reported in this unusual way.

A well-known firm in Daybrook. In 1934 one of its members received a threat to his life which, fortunately, was not carried out.

York Terrace, popularly known at Blackbird Row, was a typical turn of the century housing complex.

Miss Robinson, a highly respected teacher who ran her own private school, with one of her classes in a photograph taken between the wars.

Calverton Road School (above) with Wright Ellis in 1900 and a group of teachers at the R. Mellors School (below) sixty years later. School class photography was a popular tradition, and these two photographs give an idea of some of the changes taking place in education at the time.

Arnot Hill House and Park, on the site of the former mill, c. 1925. Rebuilt in the 1860s, it was purchased by the Council in 1914. The building was used as a hospital until 1919 when the Council used it for their offices until the area became part of Gedling.

These old buildings, c. 1955, used to house the fire brigade in its early days. The Civic Centre now stands on the site. The fire brigade was formed in 1913, when horses were used to pull the engines: there are many anecdotes relating to the catching and harnessing of the animals.

Council Events. Despite long hours of debate wrestling with problems of the day, other duties were performed such as tree planting (above) and occasional outings like this one to Wickstead Park in 1932 (below).

Outings of all sorts were greatly enjoyed as a break from the more serious business of everyday life. Unfortunately the details of these three pictures are unknown.

Watnall Gates, purchased by J. Wardle to beautify his new home on Brookfield Road. Exempt from the war effort because of their historical value, the outer pieces have been discovered still in their original position at Watnall.

The baths at the side of the library were built in 1926 and are shown here in the 1970s. This view shows the children's pool on Hallams Lane. Soon after this, the complex moved to the top of Front Street and Sainsbury's now occupies the site.

An aerial view, 1960. The Somersby Road area shows clearly the rapid encroachment on farm lands. Coppice Farm at the top of the picture was soon enveloped, and the area is now completely developed.

Rolling the soil ready for sowing, 1925. This rural scene taken on one of the fields above is now a memory.

Two views of the old Front Street, *c.* 1912. Jessamine Cottages and the old Council Offices are on the left in the top picture. The lower view shows the Baptist church and a tram sometime in the 1930s.

Front Street. A later view of the same area; changes are already obvious.

Suttons Farm, Front Street, was the last original building to be demolished. The site now stands vacant.

Top o' Town, 1958. This was the area round St Mary's church on which the original village was built. Many alterations have been made to it since.

Beacon Baptist church, Killisick, was built in 1958 to replace the original one on Front Street.

Providence Place, Coppice Road, 1955. Why this isolated row of cottages was built here remains a mystery.

Prefabricated houses on Coppice Road, c. 1955. Houses of this type were built as an emergency stopgap after the Second World War.

Front Street 'Top End' in the 1930s. Named since 1876 this area was originally part of Church Street. Many changes have occurred: flats now occupy the corner on the right and opposite is the new library and community complex.

The General Strike of 1926 saw the establishment of soup kitchens. Mr Impey, the only gentleman without a cap, and his helpers collected unsold food to make the soup for those in need.

Front Street, c. 1950, showing the building on the other side of the road from those shown in the photograph on the opposite page.

One of the many small businesses on Front Street in 1957. A smithy stood to the rear of the premises (see p. 11).

Oxclose Lane in 1920. It was here that a turnpike toll was established and disputed. Today it is a dual carriageway, developed in the late 1950s, and the lane, still there even as late as 1940, is now a memory.

Woodthorpe was developed from about 1918 as a high-quality residential area as these two photographs, taken in the late 1920s, show.

The tram terminus, 1935. This means of public transport first arrived in 1915 and was replaced by buses in 1936. The last tram started out from Daybrook Square.

A presentation of pictures by A.H. Knighton-Hammond in the library, 1946. Knighton-Hammond was born in Arnold in 1875 and studied in Nottingham and Paris, painting landscapes and travelling extensively. He retired to Misterton, Surrey, where he lived until his death in 1970.

Above: Jacoby's Factory, Sherbrooke Road, suffered two disastrous fires in 1913 and 1939. This view shows the severe damage caused by the second fire to the workers' houses which stood opposite.

Right: A public clock which originally stood outside Mount Street bus station, Nottingham, was purchased by Thurland Estates. Its use in Arnold Market Place was shortlived, however, because of senseless vandalism and it was removed in 1992.

There are many stories relating to the appearance of apparitions, from churchyard spectres and phantom cattle galloping down the main street to disappearing bus passengers, ghosts in pubs and burnt toast. This photograph was taken in 1925 from a new negative—is it real evidence?

Loyal greetings for the coronation of King George VI, prominently displayed at the Home Brewery in 1937.

This display outside the Daybrook Laundry (above) was created in 1914. A new department (below) was added by 1993. The laundry was founded by the Robinson family.

The churches organized many events such as
these, which took place between 1925 and 1955: a
procession from St Mary's church on Front Street
(left), the choir at St Paul's church, Daybrook
(above), and an unknown fancy dress group (right).

Shooting was another popular pastime and a rifle club was formed. This group photographed in 1900 was under the patronage of the Dukes of St Albans.

A less exclusive pastime was bowls. Allen-Solly's team is seen here in 1930.

In the 1930s when land at Daybrook was ceded to Nottingham, Mr Ward bought a site and set up his business which survived until his death.

Ramsdale House, Dorket Head, built for the Seely family in 1907. The house has led a varied life, having been a private residence, a school and a home for the handicapped. The site was first used earlier still, as a distribution camp by the Romans, and then by early English settlers.

Left: Samuel William Austin (known as 'Bunny' Austin) was born in Arnold in 1899. He played football for Arnold United, Norwich, Manchester United and Chesterfield. His debut was in 1924 and a year later he was capped to play against Ireland.

Below: Mystery outings were a great outlet from everyday life. This one was from Daybrook Baptist church, which celebrates its 150th anniversary this year.

The Grove Inn, Daybrook Square, opened in 1860 and is shown here about 1970. It is now a Real Ale venue. The house on the right is now being demolished to make a car park.

This cave under Cottage Row was found in 1978 when the historic building was demolished to make a parking lot. The row of houses was originally the home of the mill workers who lived there from 1790 until its closure in 1811.

The Catholic movement emerged in Arnold in 1929 and its first building is now an annex. This new one replaced it in 1962/3.

This sign erected opposite the Nell Gwyn on Oxclose lane in 1993 has instructions for an odd type of lorry—can you spot it?

Above: Another of the many corner shops which faithfully served the parish. It stood on the corner of St Alban's Road and Clinton Street, the shortest thoroughfare in the old parish.

Right: Thomas Hawksley (1807–93) was born at Arnot Hill House. He became a leading sanitary engineer with a world-wide reputation. His ideas and inventions are still in use today.

Above: High Street, once known at Back Side, *c.* 1958. All of this area was swept away to make way for the car park at the rear of the hypermarket.

Left: The New Empress on Front Street, 1958. Like the Bonington Cinema, this picture house opened in 1915 and lasted until the early 1960s. On the left is Rowbottoms the butchers. The street is now pedestrianized.

The roads into Arnold from Mapperley Plains were real country lanes in 1930 (above). The startling development over recent years is obvious in the lower picture, taken in 1990.

Surgeys Lane in 1925. The developments we see today are still some sixty years away.

Ramsdale, still rural, was the home of Joseph Whittaker (1799–1874), a friend of royalty and known as the 'Duke of Limbs'. In 1806 a chase covering 20 miles and lasting three and a half hours took place, attracting 700 horsemen and 1,000 people on foot.

Six

Rural Areas

The boundary changes of 1974 meant the end of Bestwood and Arnold parishes. Bestwood South was annexed to Nottingham, and Bestwood North along with Arnold was included within Gedling Urban District.

Bestwood Lodge, built by the 10th Duke of St Albans between 1862 and 1865 on the site of the old Royal Hunting Lodge. The estate was sold in 1940 and later was developed as a hotel and country park.

Above: Emmanuel church, *c.* 1965, was built for the Duchess of St Albans in 1865 and is now surrounded by huge housing estates.

Left: Sir J. Huddlestone is buried at the side of the church. In 1982 this 3 cwt bronze bust was stolen. It was later recovered, but in pieces.

Tradition says Charles II's favourite horse and dog are buried here. Recently this stone slab was discovered with the inscription, 'Rest here nought shall ye fear but winter and stormy weather'.

Bestwood's only cricket ground was well patronized by the Arnold men, c. 1900.

Bestwood Colliery and Iron and Steel Works created much employment and the first sixty-four houses were built to create the village. Although the industry did not last long these buildings still stand as a silent memorial to past wealth and industry.

The western entrance to the estate was named Alexandra Lodge and built in 1874. In 1992 part of it was converted into a mini museum and opened by the Mayor of Gedling and civic dignitaries of Notts County Council.

Bestwood pumping station was opened in 1874. Closed some years ago it now stands empty, despite numerous suggestions for its future use.

Bottom House Farm, 1939. The Lamin family have laboured here for many years and in 1944 William Lamin published a book entitled *30 years farming on the Clifton Park System*.

Sherwood Lodge (above) was built in 1790 and enlarged in 1845. For many years it was the home of 'squarson' (the squire and parson) Holcombe and, later, Sir C. Seely. It was finally demolished in 1974 to make way for the County Police Headquarters (below).

In the 1880s the Robin Hood Rifles spent time under canvas at Sherwood Lodge on several occasions. Various stops were made on the way. The picture above shows the 'Relief' column and below an inspection, being carried out by Col. Crealock, CB.

Despite the interruptions the farming community still carried on. This photograph dates from the 1920s.

Leapool, a road junction with its own café, c. 1950. In 1899 it was recorded that the rural part of Arnold consisted of 41 houses and 250 people north of Dorket Head, occupying 2,066 acres.

Above: Another view of Leapool, now with the roundabout added. At one time an additional ring road was proposed from Edwards Lane to emerge on the right-hand side of this picture. Redhill Arch is in the background.

Right: Sherwood Lodge School was built in 1892 on the orders of Sir C. Seely because of his concern at the long distances the children had to travel to school.

123

A class at Sherwood Lodge, *c.* 1900 (above) and patriotic displays of Empire Day in 1902 (below).

Dorket Head Farm (above), a typical farm, and the workers (below) in 1914. The farm was mentioned in a religious paper in 1760. Some years ago hand-made bricks were discovered when a back door was removed. The farm supplied the Seely family with all the essential products necessary to run Ramsdale House (see p. 107)

Although life was hard and busy, taking time to relax and put the world to rights was also indulged in, as these gentlemen demonstrate, *c.* 1914.

A new amenity near Sherwood Lodge is Burnt Stump Park where, in convivial surroundings, relaxation is the order of the day. The Lodge is shown here in 1985.

Lime Lane. During 1993 proposals were made to transform this road (running across the fields of Bestwood to Hucknall) into part of an outer ring road, but the idea was later shelved.

Dorket Head; time for reflection as once again boundary changes are being proposed.

Acknowledgements

To Gedling Borough Council, the Departments of Local Studies at Arnold and Nottingham Libraries, the *Evening Post* (Nottingham), Lakeland Stores, the artists, known and unknown, and all those people who have given permission to reproduce photographs. I apologize to anyone whose name I have unintentionally omitted. Thanks also to:

Mrs Francis • Mrs Gosling • Mrs Horsburgh • Mrs Impey • Mrs Langton
Mrs Pitt-Clark of Ipsden • Mrs Smith at Sherwood Lodge School
Miss Warwick-Parker of Sao Paulo, Brazil • Derek Brewer for typing and checking Mr B. Allen • S. Crombie • T. Hepburn • Mr Hibbert of Countesthorpe
R. Iliffe KERM • Capt. Mahy of the SA • A. Stacey of Cotgrave.

Recognition and a grateful acknowledgement is given to R. Beeton (1882–1945), whose photographic skills faithfully recorded the life and times of the parish in the first half of this century.

Finally, I dedicate this work to my wife and family for all their support.